IMAGES
*of America*

# HOT SPRINGS STATE PARK

**On the Cover:** Pictured in August 1960, the Women's Chorus processes into the annual *Gift of the Waters* pageant. The pageant commemorates the Agreement of 1896, in which the Eastern Shoshone and Northern Arapaho tribes gave Bah Guewana ("smoking waters") for the benefit of all mankind. The pageant continues to be presented during Pageant Days, the first weekend in August. (Hot Springs County Museum and Cultural Center.)

IMAGES
*of America*

# HOT SPRINGS STATE PARK

Thomas Schoenewald and
Lea Cavalli Schoenewald

ARCADIA
PUBLISHING

ISBN 978-1-4671-0672-6

Published by Arcadia Publishing
Charleston, South Carolina

Printed in the United States of America

Library of Congress Control Number: 2020950679

For all general information, please contact Arcadia Publishing:
Telephone 843-853-2070
Fax 843-853-0044
E-mail sales@arcadiapublishing.com
For customer service and orders:
Toll-Free 1-888-313-2665

Visit us on the Internet at www.arcadiapublishing.com

*To the countless people who soaked, swam, walked the terraces, built a monument, experienced a pageant, attended school, played, worked, viewed the buffalo and other animals, enjoyed a party, checked out a library book, saw a movie, performed, watched a rodeo or Demo Derby, received treatment for aches and pains, went to the fair, planted a garden, lived, picnicked, hiked, biked, stayed, got married, or made other memories.*

# Contents

# ACKNOWLEDGMENTS

The authors wish to acknowledge the assistance and encouragement of many individuals. Dorothy G. Milek was the author of the seminal effort about Hot Springs State Park, *The Gift of Bah Guewana*. Her husband, Bob Milek Sr., provided beautiful photography and original artwork. Their children graciously allowed full use of their parents' words and images. Hans Klein-Hewett, from Iowa State University, compiled a timeline of the events covered in Dorothy's book, which was used as an outline.

Rachel Moon, Nadia Cavin, the staff, and volunteers at Hot Springs County Museum and Cultural Center gave invaluable assistance. Not only did they suggest specific items from their archive, but Nadia also scanned all of the museum photographs included in this work.

Levi Shinkle's wonderful photographs can be seen on many pages in this book, particularly in chapter six. His creativity and knowledge of photography have helped present the many aspects of the park in their best light. He was willing and able to shoot anything we required and offered many excellent ideas/solutions of his own.

Barbara Tomes Vietti, geologist and state park historian, graciously read the text in this book. We are so grateful for her knowledge, frankness, and encouragement.

Kevin Skates, Hot Springs State Park superintendent, provided us with historic documents and advertising, and he was always willing to answer questions, clarify information, or share insight.

Kathy Marquis, Suzi Taylor, and the staff at the Wyoming State Archives assisted us in person in Cheyenne, Wyoming, to access the relevant images we needed. These are pictures that we could not have otherwise included here.

Many thanks for all of the stories, photographs, and kind words we received from numerous people. The state park has been, and continues to be, an important part of countless lives. We all have very personal memories from our times in the "Mile Square."

There were so many photographs and stories we simply could not include here.

Unless otherwise noted, the images in this volume were provided by Hot Springs County Museum and Cultural Center. Images provided by the Wyoming State Archives are labeled (WSA). Images donated to the museum and cultural center by the Thermopolis–Hot Springs Chamber of Commerce are labeled (C of C)

# INTRODUCTION

Long before the arrival of white explorers, trappers, and ranchers, the Big Spring was well known to Native Americans. (There were four major springs, which included the Big Spring and several small ones in the area.) The spring had many names, the best known being Bah Guewana ("smoking water"). Several Native American nations had high regard for the spring and its healing properties, and they passed down legends about its origin and location.

Chief Plenty Coups of the Crow Nation told a legend about a man named The-fringe. In a dream, The-fringe was taken safely below the waters of the Big Spring by The Person. There, The-fringe was told of the healing properties of the medicine water, which were to be used by The-fringe's village. Another legend, from the Arapaho Nation, tells of the floating feather that helped a young couple find the Big Spring. The couple was walking together in the Wind River Canyon. The girl was wearing an eagle feather in her hair that the wind carried away and onto the river. The couple followed the feather as it floated north, and it came to rest at the site of the smoking water. The couple bathed in the water and returned to their people to tell of the wonderful experience.

The springs were originally located on the extreme northeast corner of the Indian reservation in what is now Hot Springs County, in the state of Wyoming. The original reservation was the Shoshone Indian Reservation, established by the Fort Bridger Treaty of 1868. In 1878, the Arapaho tribe was placed on the Shoshone Indian Reservation. In 1938, after a court battle to settle land and resource issues, the name was changed to the Wind River Indian Reservation, where reside the Eastern Shoshone and Northern Arapaho Nations. By 1871, white settlers began ranching about 20 miles west of the spring. After 1875, a steady flow of ranchers set up homesteads in the area. Tourists as well as locals began using the waters not only for their soothing warmth but also to treat ailments such as rheumatism, diabetes mellitus, hysteria, epilepsy, paralysis, and many others. Outlaws Butch Cassidy and the Sundance Kid were said to visit the spring as they traveled between the outlaw hideouts Brown's Park in Utah/Colorado and Hole-in-the-Wall 50 miles due east of the spring. Settlers began calling the spring Big Horn. "Patients" carried rocks up nearby Monument Hill, piling them up to build their monument to prove they had been cured of their ailment(s).

In 1896, the US government purchased the 18 sections of land that contain the spring. The eastern and southern boundaries of the cession were each 10 miles ("The 10 X 10"). The springs became the property of the State of Wyoming by an act of Congress approved on June 7, 1897, becoming the Big Horn Reserve. As negotiated by Chief Washakie, Chief Sharp Nose, and Indian inspector James McLaughlin, Article II of the agreement stipulated that setting aside "the Big Horn Hot Springs for the use and benefit of the general public" and that "the Indians . . . be allowed to enjoy the advantages of the conveniences" along with the general public be a part of the treaty. This provision, insisted upon by Chief Washakie, remains today with the state bathhouse where visitors can take the waters free of charge.

Travel to the springs in the early days was quite an adventure. One could arrive by horse or wagon over the Bridger or Owl Creek Mountains from the south or along the Big Horn River from the north. Later, automobiles came over the mountains, but it was not until the railroad entered the reserve in 1910 that travel to the area could be made in comfort from the north. Non-railroad visitors from the south still had to cross the precarious Bridger Mountains until 1924, when the Park-to-Park (Rocky Mountain to Yellowstone) Highway was completed through Wind River Canyon just south of the hot springs. Now the Big Horn Mineral Hot Springs, along with the nearby town of Thermopolis, became a destination spot. Ferries across the Big Horn River to Thermopolis gave way to modern bridges. Other improvements included landscaping, water mains, hotels, sanitariums, apartments with hot water spas/baths, private swimming pools (plunges), a zoo, and elk herds. Visitors were especially fascinated by the buffalo roaming freely on the reserve because of their near extinction from overhunting. Marketing was being taken seriously, and the name Big Horn Reserve was thought to be a bit stuffy. So, in 1929, the Big Horn Reserve became Hot Springs State Park.

President Roosevelt, travelling to Yellowstone by train in 1937, made a brief stop at the Thermopolis depot, not far from Hot Springs State Park. It was after dark, but a large crowd had gathered to hear him speak. The president had been briefed on the healing waters of the Big Spring, and it was hoped he would call for a new hospital to treat ailments, including poliomyelitis. While his speech was brief, the president said he hoped that one day a hospital could be established in Hot Springs State Park that would mirror the efforts of the facility in Warm Springs, Georgia. And, after a few minutes, he was on his way to Yellowstone.

Others thought of a possible treatment center for polio victims. One such family who benefited from the Big Spring was the Gottsche (pronounced got-she) family of Rock Springs, Wyoming, about 200 miles to the southwest of the park. William and Carrie Gottsche heard of the spring and brought their daughter Marguerite to enjoy the comfort of the waters for her poliomyelitis. William, who was a rancher, died in 1939, leaving a tidy sum in his will to his wife, Carrie. Before her death in 1946, she willed much of her financial assets to the establishment of a facility in Hot Springs State Park to treat victims of poliomyelitis. She stipulated in her will that the facility should be based on the Warm Springs model. In the late 1950s, the dream came true with the establishment of the Gottsche Rehabilitation Center on the extreme southern boundary of the park. Hot water from the spring was piped to the center. As polio vaccines became successful, the emphasis for the facility as a polio treatment center became less necessary. However, Gottsche Rehabilitation Center still operates, providing service to Wyoming and the United States.

In 1925, Marie Montabe wrote the *Gift of the Waters*, a reenactment pageant depicting the Agreement of 1896. Since 1950, this pageant has been presented annually on the first full weekend of August at the Big Spring. There are two performances held on Saturday and Sunday. Local actors, singers, and Native Americans from the Wind River Indian Reservation participate in the drama.

In 1961, the idea that the spring has medicinal properties was once again brought to light when two senior high school girls, Ruth Nelson and Betsy Willison, supported by their science teacher Floyd Bass, discovered through experiments that algae from the spring was a natural antibiotic. Their conclusions caught the attention of county and Wyoming officials but not national officials. Their findings, nevertheless, won several science fair competitions and convinced many that perhaps the earlier claims of health benefits and cures from the spring were no myth.

Hot Springs State Park is unique in that it shares boundaries with the town of Thermopolis. The variety of businesses and institutions in the park may seem surprising. For instance, the west side has featured the following entities: a Civilian Conservation Corps camp, Hot Springs County Fairgrounds, Hot Springs County High School and athletic fields, Thermopolis Middle School, Ralph Witters (originally Springview) Elementary School, Carnegie Library, Hot Springs County Library, KTHE Radio, Pioneer Museum, Hot Springs County Senior Center, Pleasant View Sanitarium, Hopewell Hospital, town water treatment plant, Burlington Northern Santa Fe Railway, and the Wyoming National Guard armory. The eastern side of the park has featured many hotels, plunges, and apartments over the years. Currently, the area has two hotels, two hot water parks, the state bathhouse, the Wyoming Pioneer Home (assisted living care center), Hot Springs Health (critical access hospital), Gottsche Rehabilitation Center, and Big Horn Basin Children's Center.

Currently, the park counts about 1.3 million visitors per year. The spring was originally measured in the early 1900s to flow approximately 18.6 million gallons every 24 hours at a constant temperature of 135 degrees Fahrenheit. Today, the spring is measured by the State of Wyoming to flow approximately 2.9 million gallons per day at a temperature of 127 degrees Fahrenheit. The spring supplies enough water for the spas of two hotels, the soaking pools at the state bathhouse, and the swimming pools and spas at two privately run waterparks. There is enough left over to cascade over the colorful 200-yard-long Rainbow Terrace, eventually reaching the Big Horn River.

# *One*

# For Medicinal Purposes

The Big Spring was truly considered a wellspring for those with ailments. Many came over mountain passes and trails, like the Bridger, to seek relief and the cure for blood and skin diseases, rheumatism, and kidney complaints. The waters were said to achieve cures where other springs had failed. The spring first served the Native American population but became well known to the world by 1900.

Plenty Coups, at left, was the Crow chief who told the legend of The-fringe receiving the mineral water for mankind. After his people started traveling to the hot springs, they began dropping a bead into the water every time they passed. This was an offering to The Person. (Chief Plenty Coups State Park.)

At the turn of the 20th century, the boiling, healing medicine waters came to the surface at 135 degrees Fahrenheit at the Big Spring. More than 18 million gallons flowed per day. The water flowed down channels, formed terraces of travertine, and dropped into the Big Horn River 40 feet below.

The pristine travertine formed by the waters of the Big Spring originally fanned out in an area about a quarter of a mile from north to south and 100 yards west to the Big Horn River. The layers of travertine over the years created impressive waterfalls. In 2002, Dr. Laura Vietti, now museum and collections manager at the University of Wyoming Geology Museum, analyzed the hot springs and identified 10 different types of travertine: angel hair, tube, powder, pearl, hard white, ripple, lined, mineral, circle on circle, and plant.

Jim Bridger was an explorer, mountain man, guide, and trapper. He came to Wyoming in 1843. He blazed a trail in 1864 on the west side of the Bighorn Mountains. It was an alternative to the "Bloody Bozeman" Trail, which saw numerous warring Indian tribes. Part of the Bridger Trail goes through Hot Springs County. It was used to reach the area surrounding the springs until the railroad and other routes were established and brought more white settlers.

Jim Bridger was a longtime friend of the warrior Washakie, of the Eastern Shoshone tribe. Washakie was known as a friend to the white man. He lived for many years in close proximity to hunters and trappers in what would become western Wyoming. He became more and more prominent in the Shoshone tribe and was named as their war chief and then chief. He was also recognized by the US government as an important leader. As more and more white men came onto traditional Shoshone lands and the buffalo became scarce, the tribe was forced to hunt in the Bighorn Mountains.

Numerous thermal features have been located in the area surrounding the Big Spring. Chief Washakie even had a tub carved out of the travertine for his private use. It was fed by the Black Sulphur Spring and located just north of the Big Spring. According to Martha Schroeder, legend told of a giant black buffalo that was standing near the edge of Black Sulphur Spring crater and fell into the spring. The evil spirits made the spring stop flowing and the water to become black and bitter.

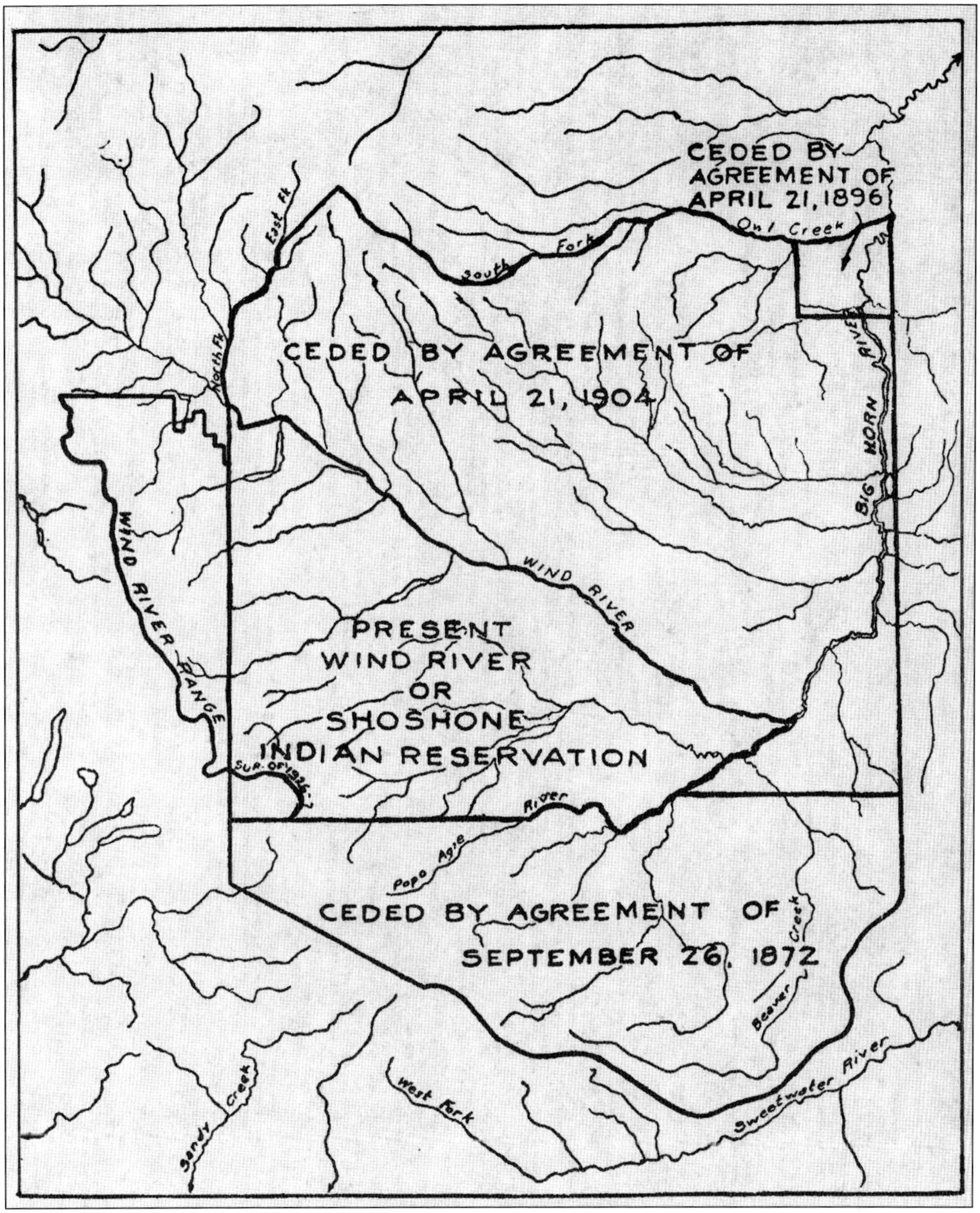


The first treaty of Fort Bridger in 1863 set the rough boundaries for the Shoshone reservation, later called the Wind River Reservation. It included the area containing the hot springs. The 44,672,000 acres covered parts of five states. The second Fort Bridger Treaty of 1868 reduced that area to 2,774,400 acres. It was further reduced by the Brunot Cession of 1872 because gold was discovered around South Pass, Wyoming.

Sharp Nose was the second chief of the Northern Arapaho Nation. In 1878, as more and more white settlers homesteaded in historic tribal areas, the tribe lost its land. They were informed by the US government that they had to "temporarily" share the Wind River Reservation with their enemies, the Eastern Shoshone. This situation continues today. (WSA.)

More and more white settlers came to the Bighorn Basin and to the area around the hot springs. According to Dorothy Milek, in 1871, John D. Woodruff built the first cabin in the entire basin, mainly to be used as a hunting camp in winter and a base for prospecting in summer. Woodruff first soaked in the springs in 1868, after a trapping expedition. He received permission from Chief Washakie to run 6,000 sheep in the area and later also ran cattle. By the 1880s, cattlemen were well established in the Owl Creek area west of the Big Spring.

Dr. Thomas Maghee was born and raised in Indiana and was an US Army surgeon. He was posted at several western forts, including Fort Brown (which became Fort Washakie) on the Wind River Reservation. In 1875, he was the first white man to analyze the healing properties of the springs. He recorded a temperature of 190 degrees Fahrenheit. In his second analysis in 1910, he recorded 135 degrees. He surmised that the Yellowstone earthquake of 1882, which changed the formation and flow of Yellowstone park geysers, also changed the Big Spring in temperature, flow, and mineral composition, making it more enjoyable for users. (WSA.)

Dr. Maghee documented his first visit to the Big Spring. He was part of an escort for a party of surveyors. The surveyors were on their way to establish the southern and eastern boundaries of the Shoshone Indian Reservation. The handwritten plaque is visible on the hill above the spring and can be viewed by hiking up the hillside. The Foote and Doneehue markers are no longer visible. (WSA.)

Army scout and later owner of the Buffalo Bill Wild West Show William F. Cody visited the springs in 1885. He had heard about the healing properties from an Arapaho warrior and asked where the springs could be found. Cody bathed his eyes to heal inflammation, which he had acquired on a South Dakota hunting trip, and was pleased with the results. (WSA.)

Outlaws were rumored to have also enjoyed the springs. Members of the Wild Bunch Gang, of which Butch Cassidy was the best known, used a canyon (Hole-in-the-Wall) 50 miles east of the springs for a hideout. Pictured are, from to right, (first row) Harry Longabaugh (Sundance Kid), Ben Kilpatrick, and George Leroy Parker (Butch Cassidy); (second row) Bill Carver and Harvey Logan (Kid Curry). The hot springs were on the route between their southern hideout (Brown's Hole in Utah/Colorado) to the Hole-in-the-Wall. Members also frequented a local bar owned by Tom Skinner, who eventually had several properties in the area. (Old West Collectors Series published by Custon Quality of El Paso.)

Wyoming was admitted to statehood in 1890. As the reputation of the springs continued to spread, settlers came to the area to bathe and to live. No permanent structures could be built on the reservation, so people squatted six miles north of the springs, past the reservation boundary. The Andersons founded a settlement, known as Andersonville, in 1890. It was located on the east side of the Big Horn River, in Johnson County. The building shown was owned by the Cochran family for many years. John Cochran remembered his parents saying that their living room was originally the bar in Andersonville and that the Hole-in-the-Wall Gang did indeed spend time there. They also told him that the gang even staged raids in Thermopolis, and they started out from the bar.

Reaching the hot springs was difficult to say the least. The area is surrounded by mountains. Stagecoaches, horses, or wagons were the only way to travel long distances. Coming from the south, travelers were forced to go over Bird's Eye Pass in the Big Horn Mountains. The trip down, over Devil's Slide, was steep and dangerous. Some stagecoach passengers even chose to get out and walk until the bottom of the slide was reached. This image shows the steep angle.

In 1891, the George Sliney family visited the springs for the second time during a cattle roundup. They were living on the Padlock Ranch on Owl Creek. They, and the Price family, wanted to soak in their own tub, as did many other visitors. People simply used pick axes, chisels, and shovels wherever it suited them. The children from both families were allowed to help dig the first tub into the travertine on the west side of the river. It would have been similar to the one shown. Tubs began appearing in numerous spots. (Photograph by Thomas Schoenewald.)

In 1894, the settlement of Old Town was founded on the west side of the Big Horn River, across from Andersonville but in Fremont County. The buildings pictured include, from left to right, the Bue Hansen home; the Hansen bunkhouse; Higgins, Bird, and McGrath Store; a butcher shop; E.C. Enderly drugstore; J.P. Nielsen blacksmith shop; Slane barbershop; and Shafer and Cunningham Saloon. (WSA.)

Jack Hollywood owned a saloon in Old Town. He later moved to a tent near the springs and owned an icehouse. He opened the Bank Exchange Saloon, otherwise known as the "Hollywood Saloon," in Thermopolis. He was accused of at least three murders and convicted of one manslaughter, but he was also known as a gambler and a "fine gentleman." Hollywood's icehouse, shown below, later became a bottling works (to bottle the mineral water and soda pop).

Dr. Julius A. Schuelke was the first permanent physician at the springs. Dr. Schuelke was so convinced that the springs had healing elements that he sent samples to a Professor Schuetzenberger in Germany for analysis. The professor returned a glowing report. Schuelke planned for a hospital, complete with gymnasium, massage, mud "electric" baths, and bathing pavilion. Sadly, Schuelke died suddenly at age 40 while on his way to promote his plans. He, along with Joe McGill, suggested Thermopolis ("Hot City") instead of Old Town as the name for a permanent settlement. He is buried at Monument Hill Cemetery in Thermopolis.

According to Dorothy Milek, Joe McGill was the first teacher at Old Town; he later taught in Thermopolis. He was known as "a brilliant educator, lawyer, former priest, and horse wrangler." He seconded Schuelke's motion at a town meeting to change the name Old Town to Thermopolis. The others at the meeting did not have "classical educations," so they "went along" with the motion. This name change was necessary in order for the new town to have its own post office.

As more people came to enjoy the waters, privacy became a priority. Loosely constructed bathhouses, using tubs dug into the travertine, helped early visitors enjoy not only the water but also the steam. Ponds were built to hold water to cool, then mixed in with the 135 degree water to make it comfortable. A gentleman stands near the earliest bathhouses, about 200 yards from the Big Spring. Care had to be taken when entering the houses in the summer, as rattlesnakes also enjoyed the shade. (WSA.)

Besides the healing opportunities provided by soaking in the water, people also began bringing bottles to fill in order to drink the water. The analysis requested by Dr. Schuelke showed that the water contained "all the minerals the body needed." Because of the numerous outlets where the water was accessible, people went to their favorite "spots." Shown is a man drawing water from White Sulphur Springs, north of the terraces near the Big Horn River. According to A.G. Lucier from Powell, Wyoming, in a 1910 souvenir brochure, "Besides the Big Spring, there are many smaller ones, of various chemical properties and any disease that will yield to the treatment of hot water, will find its proper remedy among them. The water, when bottled makes as fine a drink as any table water on the market."

As news spread of the healing waters, long lines of bathers, many ill and crippled, waited to use tubs. More bathhouses began to appear on the travertine. Permanent structures could not be built on the reservation, so M.D. Gregg of Lander, Wyoming, came up with a novel solution. The Hotel-de-Sagebrush was built of posts and poles with sagebrush arranged to form the "walls." The roof was formed in the same way, with a layer of dirt on top. Tents attached to the walls enclosed the bedrooms. Meals were also served. Gregg and unidentified guests are shown here. Later, an adjoining stable and a wooden suspension bridge across the Big Horn River were added.

R.A. Winchester came to the Owl Creek area in 1894. He began publishing a newspaper called the *Owl Creek Alert*, which later became the *Pilot*. According to Dorothy Milek, by 1896, Winchester estimated that approximately 600 people were camped near the springs in tents, covered wagons, and tepees. The camp was actually divided into sections, with each section named: Poverty Flat, Robbers' Roost, Smoky Row, Campers' Paradise, Prostitutes' Retreat, and the Indian Camp Ground. Shown are unidentified campers in one of the sections. (WSA.)

According to Dorothy Milek, the name Smoky Row was given to a section of the camp located in a draw south-southeast of the current Star Plunge. It was the first sign of humanity when travelers came to the springs from the east, and its name came from all the campfires that could be seen. Tents were pitched, dugouts dug, and the "residents" became true neighbors. Above, the draw is shown as it looks today. A cemetery was erected near the draw and was also named Smoky Row. Below are unidentified mourners. (Above, photograph by Levi Shinkle; below, original photograph courtesy of late Mrs. Ollie Cover Hollywood Coleman, rephotographed by Levi Shinkle.)

Gene Garr came from South Dakota to the springs and immediately decided to take advantage of the opportunity he saw. He wanted a facility that would hold many bathers. He got one—a tub 20 feet by 20 feet and a graduated depth of four to seven feet. It was located between the current-day Star Plunge and the state bathhouse and was covered with canvas. It also included two dressing rooms. It was cleaned every night, which was very appealing to bathers. Later, it was used as a boxing ring. Pictured above are Garr's Plunge and the terraces. The image below shows bathers in the plunge in 1899. They are identified as relatives of prominent Thermopolis resident Tom Skinner.

The Agreement of 1896 was negotiated for the United States by Indian inspector James McLaughlin. According to Dorothy Milek, when he visited the springs prior to the signing of the treaty, he remarked that the water from the Big Spring, though very hot, was not unpleasant to drink. He stated, "And with salt and pepper added (tasted) very much like chicken soup." (State Historical Society of North Dakota.)

Rep. Frank Mondell of Wyoming championed the agreement bill in the US House of Representatives. However, the US Senate was unwilling to approve the agreement because it would create a national reserve. The bill was reintroduced and approved in the next session of Congress on June 7, 1897. The State of Wyoming had already passed a bill accepting the property from the federal government. Control of the Mile Square (the area around the Big Spring as measured out in each direction from the center of the spring) was given to the State Board of Land Commissioners (later State Board of Charities and Reform).

Monument Hill and Terraces, Thermopolis, Wyo.

As more people came to the springs to relieve various ailments, celebrations for relief or a "cure" were commonplace. According to Dorothy Milek, a "Miss Avery" from Rattlesnake, Montana, had come to find relief from her inability to walk. After weeks of bathing in the water, she "recovered her health." To express her gratitude, she climbed the hill overlooking the springs and constructed a monument from rocks. The story of her effort was passed down, and the hill became known as Monument Hill, seen at left. Besides the various springs, visitors also enjoyed the numerous geological features located on the reserve. One of the most popular was called Devil's Punch Bowl, shown below. This travertine mineral formation is northeast of Monument Hill.

## *Two*

# "My Heart Feels Good"

After several years of negotiations, an agreement was settled on for transference of the area where the Big Spring and several smaller springs existed to the United States from the Indian reservation. Chief Washakie proclaimed, "I have given you the springs, my heart feels good." The agreement assured that a portion of the waters would be available for free use to all mankind. Soon, control would be granted to the State of Wyoming.

In July 1897, the residents of Thermopolis wanted to make sure they could move closer to the springs. They filed a formal petition with the state board to lay out a townsite on new property immediately adjacent to the Mile Square. The firm of Higgins and McGrath hired a surveyor, A.T. Seymour, to plat the town. The McGrath brothers are shown at left. From left to right are Jack, Denny, Thomas, and Martin. Seymour is shown below. The name "Thermopolis" was finally transferred to the new settlement later in the year.

While the townspeople waited for a final decision on a townsite, more and more visitors came to enjoy the springs. Large groups, as well as singles and couples, took advantage of the healing properties and beauty. Above, a large unidentified group gathers at the Big Spring around 1897. One gentleman even found a way out to pose on a rock. Below, an unidentified group walked to the edge of the terraces during the day to better see the waterfalls spilling into the river below.

Businesses did not wait to find out what would be allowed to operate in the Mile Square. They started operations in hopes of claiming "squatters' rights." According to Dorothy Milek, M.D. Gregg abandoned the Hotel de Sagebrush and with partner E.A. Adams built a frame bathhouse and the "shopping center" pictured above. It included a grocery, a barber, tobacco, and a snack bar on the edge of the terrace. It was called the Naturatorium and was also used for church services. One could take a soak and listen to a sermon at the same time. The Reverend Lewis C. Thompson, at left, of the Methodist Church, offered the services. (Left, Community Federated Church, rephotographed by Levi Shinkle.)

According to Dorothy Milek, other entrepreneurs established liveries, a ferry across the Big Horn, new bathhouses, a dance floor, an ice cream parlor, a blacksmith shop, and the Hot Springs Meat Market. A cable ferry is shown above; the people are unidentified. In 1898, the original Swinging Bridge, below, was built by E.A. Adams. It was three feet wide and suspended by heavy ropes. In September 1898, a total of 2,700 sheep from the David and James Dickie LU Ranch successfully crossed. Later in the fall, Al Renner of Meeteetse took 3,000 head over the bridge. A fee of 5¢ was charged to cross the Big Horn River using the bridge in this photograph. It was known as "the best footbridge in the Big Horn Basin" and was located north of the current Swinging Bridge. The people are unidentified.

The businessmen in the Mile Square wanted to have a single person oversee the newly named Big Horn Hot Springs Reserve. They requested that the state appoint a superintendent. Civil engineer V.S. Grout was hired. His engineering background prompted him to have the first property survey of the reserve. He was also needed to oversee the construction of permanent buildings. Ira Beals built Pleasant View Plunge on the west side of the river. The indoor pool is shown above. Ira and Sue Beals are pictured at left.

By 1899, the businesses on the reserve were constantly trying to update and improve their advertising. One new target group was honeymooners. Walking along the terraces in the evening, with the sounds of the waterfalls and music coming from the dance floor and various musicians in the camps, was very romantic. Young couples could even toast each other with goblets of mineral water, as this unidentified couple did around 1900.

The year 1901 brought a flurry of activity to the reserve. The Board of Charities and Reform approved the first three leases for development: Beals at Pleasant View, the Gregg & (C.C.) Weddle Sanitarium (M.D. Gregg had abandoned the Naturatorium), and the Howard Pence Plunge (later the Star Plunge, pictured above).

Another big event for the year occurred on June 3, 1901, with the opening of the two-span steel bridge over the Big Horn River. People were elated that there was finally a permanent, safe way to cross. This was considered the official opening of the reserve. V.S. Grout set strict rules for use of the bridge, including speed limits. These rules were not universally appreciated. The stereograph postcard gives a unique view of the structure.

The board came to the opening to see their pet project completed and open. They are pictured here in front of the Keystone Hotel in Thermopolis. Included in the picture (order unknown) are Gov. DeForest Richards, state treasurer George E. Abbott, state auditor LeRoy Grant, and superintendent of public instruction Thomas Tynan. During the trip, they instructed V.S. Grout to begin removing sagebrush, start landscaping, and install irrigation wells on the east side of the reserve.

Entrepreneurs were looking to make money from the water, other than by hotels, bathhouses, or swimming pools. In 1902, Charles Wallace from Meeteetse decided to use the water to make electricity for Thermopolis and the reserve. He dug a room under the terraces and lowered down a 4,000-pound waterwheel that acted as a turbine. The water ran into a hole in the ceiling and onto the turbine. In order to ensure an adequate supply of water, Wallace built a reservoir just above the plant on the travertine. However, the reservoir caused a shortage of water for the other users on the reserve, and the minerals in the water started building up on the moving parts of the generator, so the enterprise was forced to close.

The state board honored the agreement to make part of the water available to the public free of charge, so the state would have to build a bathhouse on the reserve. It was built of native stone and completed in 1903. The advertising on the roof of the building and above the door made it clear what was available. It was located near the site of the current bathhouse. Also during 1903, V.S. Grout was instructed to transplant trees to make the area more attractive.

Communication and transportation were becoming increasingly important by 1905. According to Dorothy Milek, the first telephone lines reached Thermopolis and the reserve; a right-of-way was granted to the Chicago & Northwestern (C&N), the Big Horn, and the Chicago, Burlington & Quincy (CB&Q) railroads; and the first automobile came to Thermopolis. As time passed, cars could drive directly to the spring, as seen above. The railroad construction contract was signed in 1906. Coal needed to power the steam locomotives was discovered north of Thermopolis in the towns of Gebo, pictured below, and Crosby.

W.M. Neece replaced V.S. Grout in 1905. Neece was replaced in 1907 by Jacob "The Dutchman" Paulus. During the Paulus tenure, he added concrete sidewalks, scraped terraces into terraced pools, installed a potable water line from Thermopolis, and installed wooden mineral water lines from the Big Spring to reserve lessees. Above is shown the concrete sidewalk in front of the state bathhouse. Also in 1907, William McGannon bought the lease from the Gregg & Weddle Sanitarium and changed the name to the McGannon Sanitarium and Bath House, below. All of the people are unidentified.

In 1908, Fred Holdrege, at left, bought a lease to build the Washakie Hotel. It was located on present-day Park Street. He planned a structure that was grand in scale, and it included croquet and tennis courts. Below is the completed hotel. The people on the porch are unidentified. The porch was a favorite place to sit and visit during the warm-weather months. It was advertised that "Physician, Masseurs and Masseuses in attendance; no infectious diseases will be entertained at this hotel."

Jacob Paulus continued to be forward-thinking in his position. Water pressure in the pipes on the reserve had become a real problem. He knew mineral build-up was not to blame, and he determined that steam in the pipes was the culprit. Paulus installed a 12-foot-high wooden vent pipe in 1909. It was later replaced by a 25-foot steel pipe, surrounded by a pyramid-shaped stone structure and a basin to catch the water (shown at right). The Tepee Fountain, as it is known now, is one of the most photographed features at the park. Paulus also installed a large wooden sign that advertised the Big Horn Hot Springs on Monument Hill. The sign is shown below, along with the new gazebo and various automobiles.

Railroad fever ran high in Thermopolis in 1910. During construction (shown above), a cut had to be dynamited below Pleasant View to keep the train bed level. The explosion significantly affected Fremont Spring, which fed Pleasant View. The workers are all unidentified. The people watching the work from the hill are standing near another bathtub that had been dug. They are also unidentified. Below, the first train to pull into Thermopolis is shown backing from Kirby, Wyoming, in June 1910. It had to back in because Thermopolis was the "end-of-track" until the track was completed through Wind River Canyon. The railroad line running through the reserve later became part of the Gulf-to-Sound line (from the Gulf of Mexico to Puget Sound) for CB&Q Railroad.

During this time, many grandiose structures were dreamed about for the reserve. Above is an artist's rendering of a proposed building called the Casino Plunge and Bath Scheme. It was modeled after East Coast casinos. Below is an artist's rendering of an archway for the entrance into the reserve. None of these buildings was ever constructed.

Thermopolis was becoming more and more interested in the advantages of having the reserve so close. To enhance the relationship between them, the state board allowed the city to rent part of the west side of the Mile Square. The agreement included the city building rodeo grounds and a grandstand, above, and the planting of fruit and shade trees. The grandstand and accompanying advertising were another way to bring more visitors to the Mile Square. Additionally, a small herd of elk had been calling the reserve home. During this same time, Paulus was able to obtain funds to build an enclosure for the herd, below, around Elk Hill (now T Hill).

Because of the growing importance of the superintendent and his duties, a superintendent's office (house) was built in 1911. It is pictured above. It was constructed of stone and located across the street from the Washakie Hotel, west of the current house. The people are unidentified. In December, Paulus was replaced by C.C. Weddle. As a former lessee on the Mile Square, Weddle brought a unique perspective to the job. He and his wife are shown below.

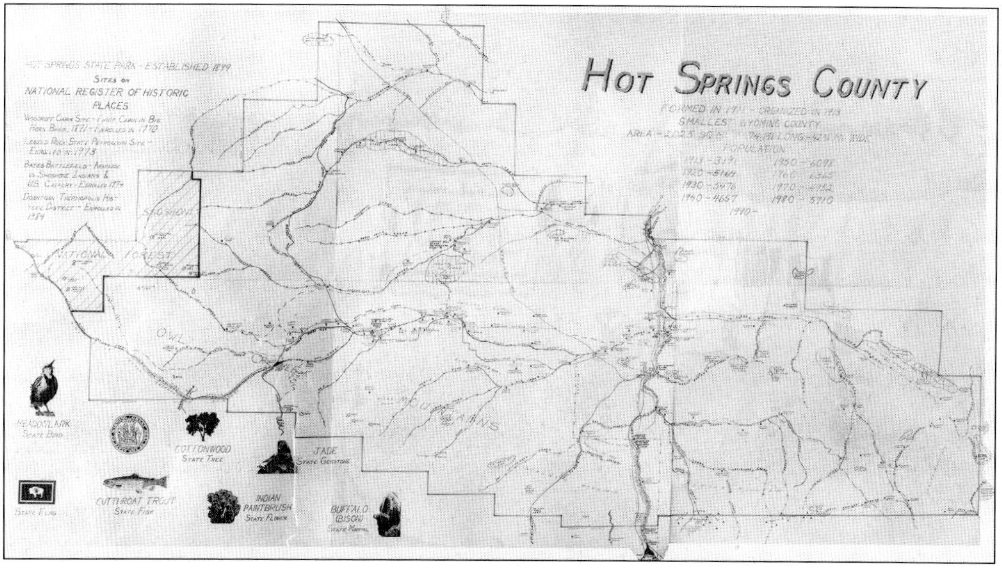

Until 1913, Hot Springs County did not exist. That year, it was organized utilizing lands annexed from Fremont, Park, and Big Horn Counties, above. Thermopolis was named its county seat. The state board approved the hiring of a public relations firm, A.O. Metz and F.M. McCormack, for the reserve. Metz operated a successful photography studio for many years and was responsible for many of the images included in this book. The Maret Apartments and House, at left (later known as Yellowstone Apartments), were built on the Mile Square. Pictured are, in no particular order, "Mrs. Monahan, Pemberton, Shaw, Maret, Clark, Don M., Margaret M., Helen."

Washakie Hotel owner Fred Holdrege went to Cheyenne (Wyoming's state capital) in 1915 to lobby on behalf of the reserve. He came back with an agreement that noncommercial buildings could be built on state property with permission. In May, Holdrege became the reserve superintendent. One of the additions he made that year was the Washakie Fountain. Its location later became known as Frank Mondell Park. Holdrege also hired a landscaping firm and a civil engineer to recommend improvements to the reserve infrastructure. The landscape plan included a metal suspension bridge.

In 1916, the Swinging Bridge was completed across the Big Horn River. Rather than a stationary walkway between the banks of the Big Horn River, the wooden walkway is suspended by metal cables attached to towers. When someone walks on it, the walkway swings and sways, thus the name was born. It is one of the few swinging bridges in the state of Wyoming. It was replaced in 1992 with another swinging bridge. The people are unidentified.

Fred Holdrege also established a zoo on the reserve. The cages, shown above, were located east across Buffalo Street from the present-day superintendent's house. According to Dorothy Milek, by the end of the year the zoo included 15 bison cows, one bull (from Yellowstone Park), elk, at least three bears, squirrels, badgers, guinea pigs, a magpie, coyotes, and a goat. The animals were hand-fed by reserve employees, and several maulings occurred. Below, the man on the left is identified as Les Thronburg.

Other animals were added over the years, including mountain lions, above, and a bobcat, right. The bobcat was caught and kept in the Wind River Canyon by J.B. White on his homestead and was later donated to the zoo. It escaped, found its way back to the canyon, and was killed by White. He had it mounted, and for many years, it served as a mascot for Hot Springs County High School, according to the book *Mystic Wind River Canyon*. It is now displayed in the Hot Springs County Museum and Cultural Center. (Right, photograph by Levi Shinkle.)

According to Kay and Necole Rush, Clare Retta Armstrong (later Axtell) came to Thermopolis in 1916 to "take care of the County Clerk's office in the Courthouse, and other typing duties." She was sickly, and her doctor said she would "not live long." She decided she would rather die in Wyoming than in her little town of Albion, Nebraska. She began taking the baths in the reserve and sitting in the steam cave at White Sulphur Spring. When Clare broke her wrist badly, she was told she "would never type again." But after soaking her wrist in the mineral mud for many hours, she was "cured." She died in 1991 at the age of 104.

More and more people were coming to the reserve to take the cure. Horse-drawn buses from the Washakie and other hotels met people at the train depot. Clare Armstrong Axtell said the hotels were always full, and guests enjoyed the porches during the day. At night, people who could not find rooms even slept on the porches of the hotels.

Dr. C. Dana Carter came to Thermopolis in 1912. He started a hospital above the Herard's Pharmacy. In 1916, with $100,000, he started construction on a three-story sanitarium and hotel. His was one of the few facilities to have an actual physician on staff. It was advertised on the postcard above as "Absolutely Fireproof" and "Where Hope Returns, and with it Health." The building included a restaurant, private rooms, a billiards and men's recreation room, and the bath and hospital department. Dancing also took place in the parlors. That same year, H.F. Rogge began work on the Antlers Hotel, below. It later became the Wanberg Spa and Nursing Home and then Rest Haven.

The Mineral Springs Apartments and House, above, were built in 1917 by S. Griffith and Owen. The photograph also shows the Tepee Fountain, Monument Hill, and the towers of the Swinging Bridge. It was located on the same row of structures as the McGannon and the Antlers Hotel. That same year, the Bungalow Café and Ice Cream Parlor, below, was built south of the Star Plunge, on the east side of the road. H.E. Rogers was the proprietor.

A man named Swanson had taken over the Washakie Hotel. By 1917, he realized that it had to be modernized. According to Dorothy Milek, Swanson and Fred Holdrege formed a new company, the Washakie Hotel and Mineral Springs Co. Inc. They planned a new $275,000 complex to include guest rooms, a dining room, a bath department, a natatorium with an indoor plunge, an outdoor swimming pool, and a coliseum in a six-story building. The only parts finished were the plunge and the bath department.

The Mile Square was a true health destination for many in the late 1910s, and visitors had a wide variety of choices, above. Clockwise from the top left are the Carter Sanitarium and Hotel, Callahan Apartments and Baths, Mineral Springs and Griffith House, Maret (Yellowstone) House, the Antlers Hotel, Washakie Plunge, McGannon Inn, the state bathhouse, Star Plunge (hidden), Washakie Hotel, and the superintendent's house. The frame houses behind the superintendent's house were used as housing for convicts, according to Clare Armstrong Axtell. These men did

maintenance work, and there were approximately 10 of them. According to Axtell, "The State Board thought they should earn their keep. When the Washakie Hotel was being built, the prisoners were used to carry hods of cement and other odd jobs. One morning when the workers went to work, the man who kept the fire going at the construction site was found dead. His death was traced back to the prisoners. After that it was decided that keeping the prisoners was not a good idea and they were no longer used in the Park." (Necole Rush.)

The United States entered World War I in 1917. That same year, the American War Mothers was formed. The Claude Branham Chapter in Hot Springs County, pictured above, included, in no particular order, (first row) Laura Hamilton, Stella Houston, Blanche Bivin, Edna Price, and Catherine Richards; (second row) Mary Valenti, Mary Daniels, Nerodine A. Suylandt, Hattie Anderson, Margaret Price, Karoline Febinger, and Dora McGrath; (third row) Mrs. Bertie Ray, Annabelle Shoop, Mattie Maret, Marie Varney, Grace French, Alice Wertz, Luanna Cover, Margaret Simpson, Laura Schickley, Elizabeth McQuire, Clara Callaway, Mary Brewer, and Bertha Armour. The rest are unidentified. When the soldiers came home, a huge picnic was held on the reserve, below. A portion of the reserve west of the Washakie Fountain was named after Walter Haynes, the first soldier from Hot Springs County lost in World War I. (Both, WSA.)

In 1918, James Callahan built the Callahan Hotel and Apartments across the street from the Carter Hotel and at the east end of the steel bridge. Callahan was a professional bricklayer who made his own bricks in a kiln he built on-site. The native soil he used gave the bricks a unique yellow color. He obtained a 98-year lease and employed several nurses and a masseur for his guests. Dr. P.W. Metz bought the property in 1921 and renamed it the Plaza, above. Also in 1918, Dr. A.G. Hamilton opened the Hopewell Hospital, below, on the hill above Pleasant View. It cost $120,000 and contained 60 rooms. According to *Hot Springs: A Wyoming County History*, the hospital's advertising contained the following: "Owing to the elevation of the building, and its isolation from the city, the danger of contamination from pus germs is reduced to a minimum."

Another plunge, the Washakie (above), was built in 1918 by Fred Holdrege. A large outdoor pool and a dance pavilion were later added. Many people later reminisced about the ring in the indoor pool. It was metal and attached to a long rope hanging from the ceiling. A person could swing from one side to the other, over the pool, by kicking off the walls. Holdrege ran for the Wyoming Legislature in 1918 and won a seat in the state house. Since he was a state appointee, this was highly questionable. The next year, his father-in-law, Colonel Sliney, at left, replaced him as superintendent. Sliney then hired Holdrege as his assistant superintendent.

# *Three*

# Fame Comes to the Springs

The new City of Thermopolis and the State of Wyoming wasted no time in promoting the springs, not only for medicinal purposes but also for recreational opportunities and the beauty of the Big Horn Reserve. An early brochure beckoned all to enjoy the area: "Thermopolis and the Big Horn Hot Springs are located at an elevation of 4,350 feet. They are on the Yellowstone Highway which forms a long link of the great Park-to-Park Highway system that is being worked out by the Government to connect up all the National Parks of the Rocky Mountain and Pacific Coast. . . . Cutting through the Owl Creek Mountains just south of Thermopolis is the Wind River Canyon. The scenery in this gorge is unsurpassed for grandeur. The Burlington railroad traverses this canyon and in the not distant future the Yellowstone Highway will be built through it as well."

Yellowstone Park had allowed automobile traffic in 1915, so more visitors were traveling through the Big Horn Reserve. The Yellowstone Highway from Denver, Colorado, to Yellowstone was established about this time but had varying levels of quality along the way. Perhaps the most difficult section was over the Bridger Mountains into Thermopolis. Several trails were said to be marked with yellow stones to indicate the route, but each had its own challenge, such as steep grades, blind corners, ruts, and narrow roadways. Above is part of the early Yellowstone Highway along Buffalo Creek before entering Thermopolis in 1919. Also in 1919, the Carnegie Corporation provided a grant of $12,500 to build a county library, below. That money was in addition to $2,497 from the county. It was in the southwest portion of the reserve.

Throughout his tenure with the reserve, Fred Holdrege was known for acquiring funding for various projects. In 1920, he wanted money to replace the steel bridge, but none was available. He then worked with state highway engineer Donald S. McCallum to designate a state highway through the reserve to qualify for federal funds. The new bridge, above, was completed in 1922. The Callahan Apartments are on the left, and the Carter Hotel is on the right. More and more large gatherings were held on the reserve, with the new bridge welcoming them in. The large group shown below is meeting near the gazebo.

The Star Plunge added a dance pavilion in front of its building in the early 1920s. Large crowds attended these popular evenings, as seen above. The plunge itself continued to be a popular recreation spot. The unidentified swimmers below enjoyed swimming in both the shallow and deep ends of the pool as well as using a series of rings and trapezes while spectators watched from two levels of balconies. The indoor pool has been in continuous use since 1901, although the building surrounding the pool has been updated many times.

The chamber of commerce donated $5,000 to build the first city-run campground on the reserve (above). It was located near the present-day football field and was called the Welfare House and Auto Campground. One advertisement read that it was the "Pleasure spot of Wyoming's Resort City." By the fall of its first season, 3,500 cars had registered. The Campfire Girls of Hot Springs County were highly active during the 1920s. Those pictured below include the state director of Campfire Girls, Blanch Hicks; Marjorie Sisk; M. Smith; Susie Drake; Evelyn Hunter; Vera Jones; and June Garrison. The adult guardian was Nellie G. Hodgson, an eighth-grade history teacher who taught in Thermopolis for many years. Here, the girls are planting flowers at the Carnegie Library.

Colonel Sliney was replaced by John Divine, pictured at left. However, Fred Holdrege continued to be successful in obtaining more funding for the park and was granted $90,000, which included $50,000 for a new state bathhouse. The new bathhouse, below, which contained 22 tubs and 3 shower baths, averaged 100 people per day. Careful records were kept of the number of visitors, and the time people could soak was regulated. Those with physical disabilities were given priority. The new bathhouse was built in the Greek Revival style and located on the site of the first bathhouse. The people are unidentified.

The new Thermopolis High School was built on the reserve in 1921 (above). It was relocated from the old Hill School site to the site of the present-day auditorium. In later years, it would be referred to as the "Old High." Elementary, music, and vocational education classrooms were located there along with a study hall and an auditorium. People could stand near the north steps of the new high school and look across present-day Park Street to see the buffalo and elk on the reserve. They could also walk over to the fence for a closer look, as shown below. The people are unidentified.

According to Dorothy Milek, an invasion of crickets and numerous downpours caused massive flooding on the reserve in 1923. The extent of the damage is shown above. The next year, the area around the Big Spring became known as "The World's Largest Mineral Hot Springs," but it is not known who coined that phrase. Later, the old wooden sign was replaced by white rocks painted and arranged on Monument Hill (shown below). In 1929, the name of the reserve was officially changed to Hot Springs State Park. The word "park" made it sound more "inviting," according to some.

In 1925, a pageant was written by Marie Montabe, shown at right. She wanted to commemorate the giving of the healing waters to all men. Shown below, it was called the *Symbolic Indian Pageant: Gift of the Waters* and was performed at the Big Spring. It was presented in October of that year by a cast of Native American dancers and singers. They were joined by several local dignitaries, and there was a large group of spectators looking on.

The swimming pools were home to many bathing beauties in the late 1920s. Pictured above at the Star Plunge are, in no particular order, Alice Dvarishkis, Mary Louise Axtell, Ruth Owens, Gertrude Ham, Bernice Shaffer, Beth Jones, Ercile Thompson, Persilla Omenson, Inez Fuller, and Irene Richmond (two are not identified). Below, tour buses sponsored by the Thermopolis Chamber of Commerce brought train passengers to visit the state park in the early 1930s. The passengers are unidentified.

By the 1930s, the Tepee Fountain (above) had grown to a height of 32 feet. Other changes in the state park included the closing of Pleasant View, a name change for Hopewell Hospital to Thermopolis General, and a push to open a veterans' hospital in Thermopolis. At the Washakie Hotel, a new manager took over for Fred Holdrege. The Arnoldus Family Orchestra, below, was hired to play at several dances at the hotel's pavilion. Dr. Arnoldus was a chiropractor for the Washakie bath department. Included the photograph in no particular order are Tim Fraser, Thelma Arnoldus, and Wesley Arnoldus.

In the 1930s, during the Great Depression, funding for the state park dropped dramatically. Because of the loss of funds, advertising for the park was also cut. The *Thermopolis Independent Record* suggested that the state should properly develop and advertise the springs or turn them back to the federal government. According to Dorothy Milek, in 1935, John Parker replaced John Divine as superintendent and fired nearly his whole staff. Parker was told to open the bathhouse on Sundays and holidays. Then he was told to stop, as it was hurting businesses. Also in 1935, the Civilian Conservation Corps (CCC) camp, above, was built in Elk Park, where the present-day National Guard armories are located. The CCC was formed to help young men have employment during the Depression. During their time in Thermopolis, the CCC boys, below, "constructed parking areas, new roads, fountains and fences," according to Milek. (Below, WSA.)

The CCC was replaced in 1937 by the Works Progress Administration (WPA) crew. Their main area of expertise was improvement of infrastructure. Many of these men were laid-off miners from Gebo and Kirby. The man above is shown building the Pioneer Museum, which stood where the current Ralph Witters Elementary gym is located. One of the enduring WPA projects was the stone wall surrounding the rodeo grounds. Well-known stonemason Alex Halone, at right in a later photograph, was a crew chief for the WPA workers.

One of the new hiking/bike trails in the park is the Quarry Trail, which passes the remains of a rail line, a dilapidated coal cart, and a cement base. The photograph at left shows the rail line, which was used in the quarry that was at one time located in the park. It is unknown how long the quarry was in operation. The crusher, below, could have been located on the cement base. The photograph is labeled as "in the State Park. The crushed rock was used in buildings and on the graded roads in the Park." (Left, photograph by Levi Shinkle; below, WSA.)

An effort was started to have a national hospital for the treatment of infantile paralysis (polio) located in Hot Springs County. Because of the difficult financial situation during the Depression, the federal government was awarding monies to local governments. It was hoped that the polio hospital would qualify for this assistance. US president Franklin Roosevelt, also a polio victim, was invited to visit the springs and see the similarities to the president's Warm Springs, Georgia, institute. His special train stopped at the Thermopolis depot at 9:00 p.m. on September 24, 1937, for 15 minutes. He made brief remarks about the importance of supporting the Infantile Paralysis Foundation and then saw the hot springs lit up, at right, as the train continued to Yellowstone Park. A bottle of mineral water was provided for the president by Thermopolis mayor Frank Milek, pictured below. The hospital was never built.

In 1938, Noah Kirby, left, became superintendent. In addition, a "hold up" marketing campaign was started. Thermopolis women "held up" the train, handed out pamphlets about the state park, and gave rides to and tours of the park. In 1938, a new city school for grades five through eight (below) was built on the site of today's bus hub. It later became Thermopolis Middle School, continuing to house grades five through eight. It was demolished in 1998. In 1939, a model of the Big Spring and Monument Hill was taken to the Golden Gate International Exposition, the world's fair in San Francisco. New marketing efforts for the state park continued to evolve.

# *Four*

# SURVIVAL?

The Great Depression and World War II forced America to rethink its values. Before 1929, the Mile Square had enjoyed a steadily growing stream of visitors. Then the stream practically dried up, as people's finances changed drastically. That situation continued through World War II, as America came together to help on the home front, and travel was curtailed to make sure the effort had all the raw materials it needed. Because of the shortage of revenue, the businesses and infrastructure in the park began to fall into disrepair. This situation caused many in Thermopolis to question whether the reserve should be closed. Some even suggested that the park should be turned back to the US government. After the war, materials and labor became available again, and more attention was given to the needed repairs. New types of businesses were also allowed to obtain leases and to open.

The 1940s brought a world war and a real downturn in the number of tourists who visited the Mile Square during those lean years. Other significant changes were also seen. Several innovative marketing efforts were tried, including a new sign at the entrance to the park, at left. It contained the following information: "You are now at Thermopolis and the World's Greatest Mineral Hot Springs: Swimming Pools, Bath Houses, Dancing Every Night, Hot Water Lakes, Boiling Springs and Falls, Geyser Park Drives, Mountain Climbing, Zoo of Rocky Mountain Animals, Big Hotels and Fine Apartments." Wyoming governor Lester C. Hunt, below, came to Thermopolis and spoke to a group of residents in the park, west of the Carnegie Library. Later in the decade, he appointed an advisory committee to act as a liaison between Thermopolis and the state board.

In 1941, the Antlers Hotel was severely damaged by fire, shown above, and the furniture was brought outside, including the piano. It could not be repaired due to a materials shortage. The next year, safety and attractiveness were enhanced around the Big Spring, shown below, with the addition of the rockwork and lighting done by the WPA workers at the request of Noah Kirby. However, he stated in 1944 that the reduction in tourists might be a reason to close the park.

At Thermopolis High School, the students had numerous opportunities to excel in academics and other activities. Pictured above, the starting five for the 1941 Thermopolis Bobcat basketball team are, from left to right, Serfin Rey, Bob Hatafield, John Pilch, Joe Galovich, and Jack Rae King. Pilch went on to play at the University of Wyoming and was the leading scorer during his career there. He was drafted into the NBA by the Baltimore Bullets and played one season with the Minneapolis Lakers. Below, in 1948, Duke Bolich ran hurdles for the Bobcats. The track was in front of the grandstands at the rodeo grounds because there was not a track around the football field at the high school.

Hopewell Hospital (Thermopolis General) closed in 1942, and a committee was formed to try and reopen it. Above are five unidentified nurses in front of the facility. It reopened in 1944, and Hot Springs County took over control in 1946. An Army-Navy hospital was also proposed by the chamber of commerce in 1943, but nothing came of that. In 1944, Carrie Gottsche died. She left a significant amount of money in memory of her daughter Marguerite, shown below, who had suffered from polio. Carrie Gottsche and her husband, William, sought many treatments for Marguerite, but she seemed to find the most relief in Thermopolis. The money Carrie Gottsche left was to be used for the "rehabilitation of all handicapped and disabled persons" in a facility located in Thermopolis.

In 1944, the Antlers Hotel was rebuilt and became the Wanberg Spa, shown above. It later became the Rest Haven Nursing Home. In 1945, Bud King, pictured at left, took over the superintendent's job for Noah Kirby. Two legislators attempted to introduce a bill to build a Wyoming "old folks' home" in the park, but it failed. A second attempt was made in 1946. Governor Hunt vetoed the bill, but the legislature overrode him. In 1946, the elk herd escaped from the park, and there were very few buffalo left. The war years had taken a severe toll on the funds available to feed these animals and those in the zoo. Any animals that were left (other than the buffalo) were set free.

By the mid-1940s, rodeo had become immensely popular. Tim McCoy, pictured at right, who owned a dude ranch west of Thermopolis, was a famous movie star. He came back to Thermopolis to serve as grand marshal of the annual Labor Day Rodeo Parade. The calf and steer ropers shown below are, from left to right, Hyde Merritt, Buster Hayes, unidentified, Lourie Hayes, unidentified, and Justin McCarthy.

In 1947, Scott Taylor, pictured at left, replaced Bud King as superintendent. Taylor began an effort to get community input for improving the Mile Square. He even started a newspaper column that reported news from the park. According to Dorothy Milek, he asked the state engineer for recommendations and wanted regular inspections by the State Department of Health. The bathhouse was closed for renovations, and a new fountain, shown below, was completed on the west side of the river. It is located by the present-day chamber of commerce. In addition, $6,000 was donated to refurbish the rodeo grounds.

Scott Taylor purchased the Star Plunge lease in 1948 and added an outdoor pool in 1950. The park continued to be used by a variety of groups, including the Boy Scouts. They are shown above at a Scout Jamboree on the rodeo grounds in May 1949. Construction began that year on the Wyoming Home and Hospital for the Aged. A legislative committee decided that knowledge of the park was "lacking." The local Jaycee organization put up signs around town, while the chamber of commerce put up signs around the state, calling the park the "Health Center of the West." In 1950, the high school rodeo queen and her court, shown below, reigned over the annual competition. They are, from left to right, unidentified, Daisy Hooley, Twila Rathbun, Queen Jewel Duncan, unidentified, Katy Jane Sanford, and Barbara Bender.

The *Gift of the Waters* pageant was revived in 1950, with author Marie Montabe directing. More than 100 local women participated in the chorus. Gift of the Waters Inc. was formed in 1951. A dedicated group of local citizens had become participants in the annual event. One of them was Virginia Mortimore, shown at left. Also in 1951, the Wyoming Home and Hospital for the Aged (later the Wyoming Pioneer Home) opened. The grand opening was attended by Wyoming state officials. They are, from left to right, Secretary of State Arthur Crane, unidentified, superintendent of public instruction Edna Stolt, Gov. Frank Barrett, unidentified, and state auditor Everett Copehavener.

According to Dorothy Milek, Governor Barrett proclaimed Hot Springs Park Day as an annual event in Wyoming in 1952. It remained so until it was decided to rotate Wyoming State Park Day between all Wyoming state parks. This caused some to talk about the park becoming more valuable as a recreational destination rather than a health destination. Above, a large group at the Carter Hotel assembled for a speaker. At right, the Tepee Fountain was still a popular spot to stop for a photograph. An unidentified group poses on the stone wall around the formation. The wall was later removed.

In 1952, a meeting was held in Governor Barrett's office regarding the use of the Gottsche estate. William H. Gottsche is shown at left. According to the *Casper Star-Tribune*, "The groups attending the meeting included: the State Public Health Department; the Rock Springs National Bank trustees; the Division of Crippled Children; Department of Education; Thermopolis Gottsche Memorial Committee; medical advisory committee; the Legislative Interim Committee; and architects. Also attending were Edwin V. Magagna and Kenneth G. Hamm, Rock Springs attorneys for the estate." Below, construction began on the facility a few years later in conjunction with a new hospital.

The Wyoming Home and Hospital for the Aged was expanded in 1953. Roy Montgomery donated $250,000 for a wing dedicated to care for the blind. A "health pool" was added to the back of the bathhouse. Twenty-five acres were added to the east side of the park for a buffalo pasture. In 1955, George Fogelsonger, shown at right, became superintendent. That year, a new superintendent's home was built, shown below. (Below, photograph by Bob Milek Sr., rephotographed by Levi Shinkle.)

In 1957, Hot Springs County senator Joe Rushin sponsored a bill to allow a 99-year lease to build a new hospital. Also, two new businesses were granted leases in the Mile Square. The Rio Drive-In, shown in the lower left corner above, was owned by Fred and Ann Curtis. The drive-in sold many iconic movie treats, including the "Green River" drink. The Greater Learning Center Area occupies the site today. KTHE Radio, 1240 AM, was owned by Hugh Graham, shown in the middle below, and his partner, Bill Peterson. Also pictured on the right is Sue Gebhart. The other person is unidentified. The station was located near the football field, north of the present-day Hot Springs County Senior Citizens Center Inc. According to Dorothy Milek, there was concern at this time that structures such as these on the west side of the park were "built contrary to the original intent of the Indians." A later ruling by the state attorney general said that "the businesses of Curtis and Graham were legal, since they were for the pleasure of the public." (Both, C of C.)

In 1958, construction on the new hospital and the rehabilitation center began. The new Hot Springs County High School, shown above, opened on Park Street. The architecture was very typical of the schools built at that time. It housed the second-largest high school gymnasium in the state for many years. The building it replaced became the "Old High." High school rodeos continued to be popular. An unidentified bareback bronc rider is shown below.

The popular *Gift of the Waters* pageant brought many visitors in the summer. Above, Felix Washakie Perry portrays his great-grandfather Chief Washakie with his hands stretched out over the Big Spring. This gesture signified the giving of the waters. He played this role in the pageant for many years. People also continued to come to the Mile Square for their health. The Plaza, pictured at left, advertised: "Fountain of Health. Drink this highly-mineralized water. You'll have good Luck and good health. Water from . . . World's Largest mineral hot springs. Flowing 18,600,000 gallons daily. Contains sixteen different minerals." The signs in the windows read, "Massage, vapor, mineral baths." The women are unidentified.

School outings to the park were also popular, as seen above. Tall metal slides, teeter-totters, and merry-go-rounds were all common playground and park equipment at the time. Learning to swim in the mineral water was a common summer activity. Below, at the Washakie Plunge, a group swimming lesson is taking place; all age groups participated at the same time. A large outdoor pool was added in the 1930s. All the people pictured are unidentified.

Ted Nelson, shown at left, became superintendent in 1959. The state board had allowed free bathing for Wyomingites at the state bathhouse for almost 20 years. It was then opened to the public. Nelson was faced with some backlash, but it did subside. A new sign at the park entrance, seen below, also appeared this year. It advertised "mineral baths and treatments, swimming, hotels, apts., snack bars, dining room, shady picnic and camp ground, see large buffalo herd."

The Hot Springs County Memorial Hospital and Gottsche Rehabilitation Center building opened in 1959. Shown above are, from left to right, Lorne Fogelsonger, Donnell Anderson (hospital administrator), and Dr. Benjamin Gitlitz in the hospital operating room. At right is an unidentified physical therapist at Gottsche. The mineral water was piped in for whirlpool baths.

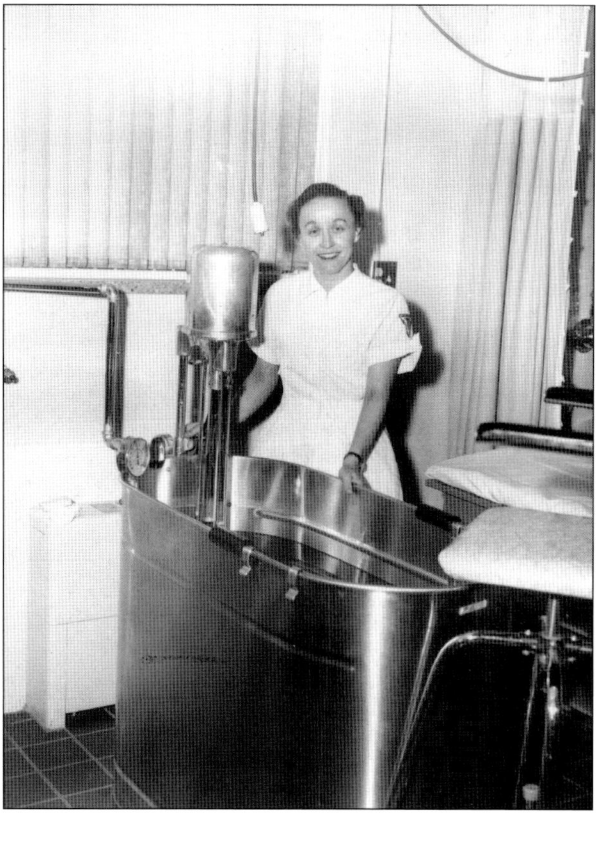

The last remnant of the CCC camp barracks, above, had been moved to the corner of Railroad (now Senior) Avenue and Park Street. It was renamed the Scout House and was used for many years for Boy and Girl Scout functions, dances, and other activities. It was later demolished. The Thermopolis Shrine Club sponsored various activities in the community for many years, particularly those for children. The Shrine Circus was a popular annual event at the rodeo grounds, shown below. All people are unidentified.

# *Five*

# Bigger and Better

The State of Wyoming took a renewed interest in Hot Springs State Park. Committees were formed to study the infrastructure and to make recommendations. Almost all the original buildings were demolished, leaving only the Plaza and Star Plunge. Both sides of the park were now changing. Additions on the east side of the Big Horn River included a new water park, a hotel, a hospital, a rehabilitation center, a home for the aged, new superintendent quarters, and a center for children with behavioral concerns. West of the river, the park had a new elementary school, library, radio station, senior center, National Guard armory, and baseball fields.

"Red" Alexander, above, was the caretaker at the Pioneer Museum for many years. Schoolchildren stopped in to see him after school, and he was always happy to answer questions and show them around. The museum was located next to Springview Primary School, which housed kindergarten through third grades. Shown below is kindergarten teacher Bette Cavalli with her morning class in 1966. The Pioneer Museum became the Hot Springs County Pioneer Museum in 1963. It was relocated and the name changed to Hot Springs County Museum and Cultural Center in 1977.

Ted Nelson opened a temporary campground, shown above, on the peninsula underneath the terraces in 1960. It was closed the next year because funds were not approved for sanitation improvements. The Park Service Committee made its own plans to reopen it, and the state board conducted a study. The *Thermopolis Independent Record* demanded a definition of what constituted an acceptable "camping" enclosure. Eventually, the state attorney general ruled "all trailer campers were acceptable." The citizens of Thermopolis opened a free campground north of the park, where the Sacajawea Spring (later renamed the Scotch Plunge) was located, shown below. It eventually became the Fountain of Youth. The people are unidentified. (Below, Eddie and Vera Hausauer.)

The Thermopolis community Amateur Athletic Union (AAU) and the high school boys swimming teams practiced and held meets at the Washakie Plunge for many years. Shown above are high school swimmers, adults, and coach Jack Beard (in white T-shirt) in 1960. After the plunge was demolished, the teams moved their practices and meets to the Tepee Spa. The high school band, below, presented marching routines at various football games. Even after a snowstorm, the band, drum majorette, and baton twirlers still played, marched, and twirled for the hometown crowd's pleasure. They are shown in a trademark *T* formation in the early 1960s. (Above, C of C.)

The *Gift of the Waters* pageant includes numerous parts, and many Native Americans sing and dance throughout the show. The women's chorus chants two songs, and "Preparation for the Gifts," above, shows the women's chorus linking arms behind backs and doing a round dance while chanting the song-prayer to Dama Upa ("Our Father") in 1960. Below, a Native American archer shoots an arrow to send a message to the Great Spirit. The participants are unidentified.

Don Tippets was the Hot Springs County extension agent for the University of Wyoming for decades. In the 1960s, he assisted with the International Farm Youth Exchange (IFYE) program. Students visited other countries for approximately one month and observed a farming or ranching operation. Here, Tippets is shown with an unidentified student who was visiting Thermopolis. They are standing in front of an elk antler tower in the park.

Showing animals at the annual Hot Springs County Fair has been part of 4-H and Future Farmers of America (FFA) members' lives for decades. In 1962, Jim Wilson showed the Grand Champion Steer and Grand Champion Hereford Heifer at the fairgrounds.

In 1961, Ruth Jackson (left) and Betsy Willison (right), pictured above at the Big Spring, entered the Wyoming State Science Fair. Their project centered on the viability of using the mineral water to make an antibiotic. The project, which involved the isolation of mold spores from the hot mineral water, received top honors. According to the *Thermopolis Independent Record*, the work showed the spores inhibited the growth of two "streps," two "staphs," and also "E-col." The girls' biology teacher that year was Floyd Bass, below. He was Wyoming Teacher of the Year for 1961 and One of Ten of America's Best in 1962. (Above, Ruth Jackson Betz.)

Ruth Jackson and Betsy Willison were aided by Jake Poole, a Hot Springs County Memorial Hospital laboratory technician. Pictured above are, from left to right, (seated) John Bury; (standing) Donnell Anderson, Jake Poole, and Darrell Hunt (manager of Gottsche). Poole had been contacted by the state health department, which made an inquiry about the safety of the mineral water. He was asked to do further testing, which led to the girls' project. Poole and Floyd Bass decided which bacteria was to be tested, and Poole helped the girls get equipment and chemicals for their experiments. Ruth Jackson, shown below with Bass, was the only one who was allowed to attend the Wyoming State Science Fair (only one person could enter a project). Because of her success at the state level, Jackson was invited to attend the Wyoming and Colorado Bi-State Fair. (Above, C of C; below, Ruth Jackson Betz.)

The 1960s brought new marketing strategies. Above, a travel trailer encouraged people in other locales to "See the Whole World's Largest Mineral Hot Springs." It was parked in front of City Plumbing & Heating, owned by Carl and Marguerite Packer. Below, a new sign on Broadway Street pointed tourists toward the park.

In the 1960s, the Carter Hotel was a destination for social events of all kinds, including wedding receptions, luncheons, banquets, bridal and baby showers, and fashion shows. Model Florence Hopcus, daughter of Eleanor and Stanley Hopcus, is shown above in the sunroom. Blanche Todd is in the background, second from left. The other woman unidentified. The Carter Hotel was managed for many years by Eddie and Wanda Nordquist, pictured below. They managed the Plaza as well. (Both, C of C.)

In 1963, Scott Taylor installed the Screamin' Mimi ride in the outdoor pool at the Star Plunge, above. A person sat on a wooden sled at the top of a track and rode down. The goal was to skim across the water all the way to the end of the pool before the sled sank. The name came from the way the girls screamed as they raced down the track. Below is a free pass for the Screamin' Mimi.

Wyoming governor Jack Gage, above, attended a local VFW function in the early 1960s. According to Dorothy Milek, the governor had announced that the springs were "the most famous water in Wyoming." Bottled water was sent to a luxury hotel in Boise, Idaho, to be used for drinking, and it was also mixed with water from all 50 states into a swimming pool. Throughout the park's history, photographers have found inspiration in the scenery. A winter scene, below, is from the same time period. It shows a winding street in the park. (Below, Brenda Ralston.)

In 1962, the Daughters of the American Revolution dedicated a monument at Smoky Row Cemetery, right. Pictured are, from left to right, Anna Peterson, Nell Hodgson, Gloria Russell, and Altha Pyle. According to Dorothy Milek, that same year Ted Nelson asked the National Park Service for a study and report on the east side of the river. The recommendations were as follows: "Creation of a Master Plan, removal of several buildings to make the Park more parklike, removal of several buildings in poor condition, and the creation of a long-term employee as manager (not a political appointee), in order to allow for more long-term planning." In 1963, Bob Johnstone, below, was named superintendent.

Wyoming governor (and later senator) Clifford Hansen, above center, visited the park in 1964. The others in the photograph are unidentified. According to Dorothy Milek, Hansen announced plans for a "new entrance and information office in the shape of a tepee." The chamber of commerce building, below, was completed in 1966 and is still in use today. The building and accompanying sign show the familiar tepee motif of the park. The state board contacted public health and fire officials and requested assessments of existing park buildings. Plans were made to demolish several of them.

In 1966, several original structures were demolished: the Maret, Hot Springs Apartments, and Mineral Springs Apartments. According to Dorothy Milek, Bob Johnstone also asked for funds to build a new bathhouse. He stated that the old building was so run down no heavy equipment would even be needed to take it down. The steam and minerals in the water had greatly weakened the mortar in the walls. According to Milek, a "double walled, specially treated concrete Bath House," above, was opened in 1967 and is still in use today. Renowned artist Rupert Conrad, right, painted a mural for the new structure. That same year, the Wyoming Legislature allocated federal funds to be used in the park for the encouragement of new investment.

A lease was granted to Darrell Hunt in 1967 to build a new swimming pool near the bathhouse. He worked with the Thermopolis Development Corporation on a new design, and the Tepee Spa, pictured at left, was built that year. It was constructed with a plexiglass and redwood-beamed roof covering swimming, soaking, and wading pools and other amenities. It burned in 1975 and was rebuilt without the tepee architecture. In 1969, several more hotels were demolished: the Antlers, Washakie, and Carter. In 1971, the Holiday Inn of the Waters, below, opened. The park's familiar tepee motif was continued in the entryway.

In 1973, the US Army Reserve 224th Engineer Battalion came to Thermopolis to "practice building." Its major objective was construction of a permanent home for the Northwest Board of Cooperative Educational Services (NWBOCES), at right. Prior to that time, NWBOCES had been housed at Gottsche. This was the first time that peacetime reservists had done such work. According to the *Thermopolis Independent Record*, NWBOCES serves youth from all over the state of Wyoming, from kindergarten through eighth grade, who have behavioral and emotional disabilities. In 1973, the Hot Springs County Senior Citizens Center Inc., below, was constructed. It is still the destination for lunch, home-delivered meals, crafts, pool, medical information, homemaking services, card games, and transportation (medical trips, shopping trips, and trips to sites in Wyoming). (Both, photographs by Levi Shinkle.)

An artistic addition to the park in the early 1970s was the Floating Feather Fountain, left, located north of the Wyoming Pioneer Home. The name, from a contest won by Ruby Hanson, came from an Arapaho legend regarding the discovery of the hot springs. Created by Gerald Shippen, the statue was added in 1990 to commemorate the Wyoming centennial and the signing of the Agreement of 1896 and depicts Chief Sharp Nose, Chief Washakie, and James McLaughlin. In the mid-1970s, federal funds were used to build an outdoor pavilion, below, on the site of the old Washakie Plunge (demolished in 1969). It continues to be used today for concerts, lectures, meetings, and events such as the Hot Springs Arts and Crafts Fair and Relay for Life. It is dedicated to the memory of Bob Johnstone.

The *Gift of the Waters* pageant, now performed during Pageant Days, continues to draw large crowds to Mile Square every year during the first weekend of August. Above, Native American men and boys dance at the Big Spring. The dancer facing the camera is Larry Wagon, and second from the right is Louis Addison. The others are unidentified. At right are petroglyphs from the Legend Rock Petroglyph Site, approximately 25 miles northwest of Thermopolis. A total of 283 glyphs on 92 rock panels, some 10,000 years old, are found there. The site is under the supervision of the current superintendent, Kevin Skates, and his staff.

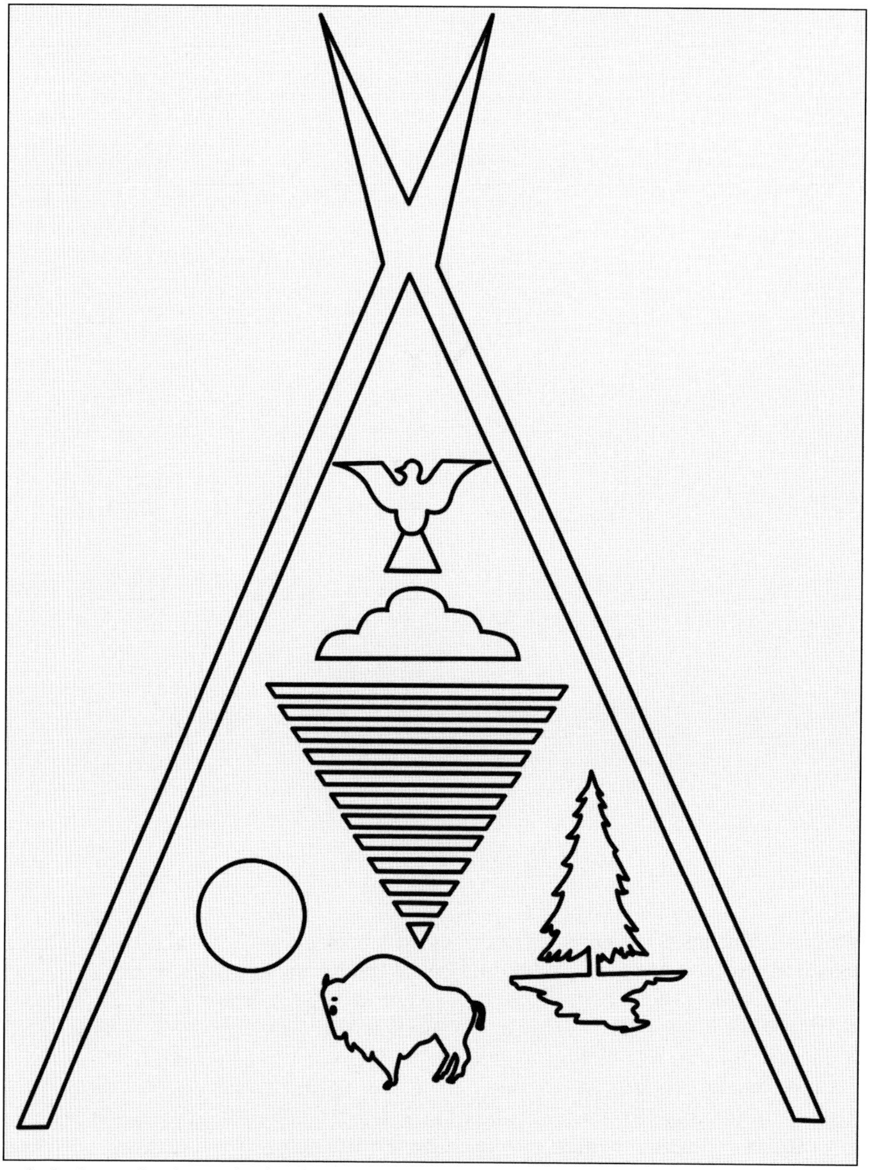

The symbols from the legend of Bah Guewana each have a corresponding color. According to excerpts from a legend told by Herman St. Clair, chief of the Shoshones, and courtesy of the *Thermopolis Independent Record*, the four corners of the world are symbolized by the yellow flying bird of the north, the green tree of the east, the red buffalo of the south, and the white circle of purity. Between these four corners of the earth is placed a cone made of 12 colored bars, spaced with the bars of white. The first four colored bars are green, spaced with the white, and stand for Mother Earth. The four red bars, spaced with the white, have the same meaning as the red buffalo, which furnished the Indians with food, clothing, and shelter. The next four colored bars are yellow, spaced with the white of purity. These yellow lines symbolize that the birds use the water below the springs to stop on during their migrations because it never freezes. The blue smoke above the cone is symbolic of the smoking water from which it derived its Indian name, Bah Guewana. The cone denotes that the water came from deep in the earth and brought to the surface health-giving elements. (Photograph by Levi Shinkle.)

# *Six*

# The Legacy Continues

Since 1980, Hot Springs State Park has continued to grow and evolve. The need to modernize has necessitated new construction and numerous additions and upgrades to existing structures. For example, water from the Big Spring is no longer cooled in open cooling ponds. The water is now piped to the Big Horn River, and pipes run under the riverbed where the hot mineral water is cooled. The cooled water is then pumped to the hotels, pools, and bathhouse. As new residents have moved to Hot Springs County and more tourists are visiting the park, they have demanded more—a better variety of hotel and motel amenities, bigger and faster slides and other waterpark offerings, more sophisticated medical care, the opportunity to hike and bike, modern schools, a place to hone skateboard skills, arts/crafts/humanities gatherings, and . . . the list continues.

Bob Johnstone retired in 1985 and was replaced by Don Lester. After Lester, the following people served as superintendent: Allan Cowerton, Ken Cundall, and Todd Stevenson. The 1980s brought continued efforts to bring constant activity to the park. Summer melodramas on the stage of the pavilion were very popular. Here. Michelle Raymond (left), Todd Eagle (seated), and Juanita Glass (right) perform. These performances always included a sweet and innocent heroine, a brave and handsome hero, and some type of evil villain who always lost in the end.

"Old High" was demolished in 1984, and in its place, the School District Administration Building was completed in 1985. The building is still in use today and contains offices, classrooms, and an 801-seat auditorium. The auditorium is the setting for concerts, plays, lectures, awards assemblies, meetings, prom grand marches, and numerous other activities.

The Carnegie Library was replaced by a new county library, pictured at right, in 1966. An addition was made to the new facility in 1986. The original library is now the University of Wyoming Extension for Hot Springs County and provides the county with "reliable, research-based information in agriculture and natural resources, consumer and family economics, community and economic development, and 4-H/youth development." The Wyoming Pioneer Home, below, is today an assisted living facility. According to the Wyoming Department of Health, it is 84,000 square feet of living space. It "promotes independent living, while offering a comfortable and pleasant home for each resident." (Both, photographs by Levi Shinkle.)

Over the years, Thermopolis service organizations have built picnic shelters in the park; the Lions Club has built two. The newer, called Smoking Water Shelter, above, is located near the Big Spring, and the older shelter is located across the street from the Star Plunge. The Kiwanis Club of Thermopolis built its first shelter, below, in 1968. Called the Washakie Shelter, it followed the tepee motif. The second shelter the club built is near the boat dock, closer to the Big Horn River. All of the shelters are in great demand from spring to fall and must be reserved in advance. They are popular for family gatherings, money-making projects, and other uses. (Both, photographs by Levi Shinkle.)

Kevin Skates, right, became superintendent in 2006, after Todd Stevenson. He has overseen the addition of many new activities and traditions in the park. Hiking and mountain biking trails, cut with assistance from the State of Wyoming, are bringing a new group of park users, and several more are in the planning stage. During Pageant Days, the Wyoming Discovery Days are held. Featured are storytellers, artists, craftsmen, musicians, demonstrations, hands-on activities for kids, and a trading post. Skates and his staff provide any needed assistance to vendors and visitors during the weekend. One of Skates's major duties is maintenance of the iconic buffalo herd, below. The herd continues to be one of the most popular features in the park. (Right, Hot Springs County Museum and Cultural Center, rephotographed by Levi Shinkle; below, photograph by Levi Shinkle.)

The previous Hot Springs County High School building was demolished in 2005, and the new structure, above, was completed in 2006. It houses grades 9–12 and approximately 200 students. Below, Springview Primary School has had several changes over the years and was renamed Ralph Witters Elementary. (Both, photographs by Levi Shinkle.)

The community baseball fields have always been in the Mile Square. A complex of smaller fields was located near the fairgrounds, and the regulation-size field was located next to the previous high school. Later, the bigger field was demolished to make room for the new high school building, and two of the smaller fields were combined to make a new regulation-size field. The whole complex, above, is now named after longtime baseball supporter Mark Whitt. Near the baseball fields is the community skate park, below. It was built in 2006, and those who use it helped raise money for the project. It includes a half-pipe, a box, a ramp, and a few rails. (Both, photographs by Levi Shinkle.)

A community project that is still used and loved today is the Play Park. A committee was formed in the early 1990s, funds were raised, a design was accepted, materials were received, and approximately 400 adults and children worked for weeks to create the park. When the Play Park started to show its age, there was talk of demolishing it. However, Guy Bjorklund, longtime businessman and community advocate, led an effort to raise enough money to refurbish it. Again, the community came out to get the job done. (Photograph by Levi Shinkle.)

A Hot Springs County native, Leroy Hayes was an athlete, teacher, and coach. He died in 2013. To honor his devotion and contributions to education and sports (especially football), the high school football field was named for him. A "100 Years of Bobcat Football" celebration was held at the field in October 2020. (Photograph by Levi Shinkle.)

Extensive remodeling was done when the Holiday Inn became the Days Inn by Wyndham Thermopolis in 2008. The facility contains 80 rooms, a restaurant and lounge, exercise rooms, hot tubs, and a steam room. (Photograph by Levi Shinkle.)

The Plaza is still in business as the Best Western Plus Plaza Hotel. It is the only hotel in the park that retains its original exterior. Several of the original apartments have been combined into suites, and a freshwater pool has been added outside. (Photograph by Levi Shinkle.)

On the site of the old CCC camp, two Wyoming National Guard armories have been built. The older one, shown in the 1960s, was used by the highly decorated A Battery 300th Armored Field Artillery. It is now used for state park storage and equipment. The newer one houses the Hot Springs County Recreation District office.

The Tepee Fountain has been welcoming visitors for 111 years. An earlier flyer from the Mineral Springs Apartments offered the following advice: "Get a pitcher of mineral water from the Tepee Fountain and use it in making your coffee or tea. Use it in all your cooking. Get the minerals into your body. Bathe in it; swim in it! Drink it. This water cures many diseases after the doctors have tried months and years and failed to cure." (Photograph by Levi Shinkle.)

The Tepee Spa is now Hellie's Tepee Pools. It offers indoor and outdoor pools, slides, and hot tubs. (Photograph by Levi Shinkle.)

The Star Plunge is the oldest continuous business in the park. It offers indoor and outdoor pools and hot tubs, a baby pool, a jumping platform, sun decks, two outdoor slides, a steam cave, a fitness and weight room, a tanning booth, a game room, snacks, and a gift shop. (Photograph by Levi Shinkle.)

Hot Springs County Memorial Hospital is now Hot Springs Health, pictured at left. It is the only critical-care facility within 35 miles. It has been undergoing a major renovation and addition project since 2018. Phase one of the addition includes a new state-of-the-art emergency area, nurses' station, patient care area, obstetrics, and surgery department. Future additions will include departments for food and nutrition, ambulatory, pharmacy, and diagnostic imaging. (Photograph by Levi Shinkle.)

The Gottsche Rehabilitation and Wellness Center has also been undergoing major changes in the last few years. It was originally meant to be a polio rehabilitation center, modeled after President Roosevelt's center in Warm Springs, Georgia. However, by the time construction was begun, infantile paralysis was being controlled by vaccines. The center has grown into a regionally recognized clinic for physical, occupational, speech, aquatic, and massage therapies, with clinics in neighboring counties. In addition, a wellness center has been added with a wide variety of fitness equipment and a climbing wall. The outside facade and inside spaces have been updated as well. (Photograph by Levi Shinkle.)

Disc golfer Frank Luna is enjoying the Greater Learning Center Area's course. It is another newcomer to the park. The disc used to play this type of golf resembles a Frisbee but is smaller and denser. It is thrown in a similar manner, but it is only meant to be thrown, not caught like a Frisbee. More than 120,000 lifetime members belong to the Professional Disc Golf Association. (Photograph by Levi Shinkle.)

Numerous couples have used the backdrop of the state park as a setting for their wedding. Angela and Eric Evenson are shown at their 2020 celebration. (Photograph by Levi Shinkle.)

People have renewed the practice of making "monuments" on Monument Hill after hiking up any of the three recently constructed Monument Hill trails. There is also a guest book to sign for proof that a hike to the top was completed. (Photograph by Levi Shinkle.)

Mountain biking is becoming more and more popular in the Mile Square. Mountain bikers Chris and Jennifer Paris are shown on the newest park trail, the Zoo Trail. It winds around the original zoo location, where the foundations of the cages and the caves where the animals were kept can still be seen. It is a shorter trail, about one half-mile in length. (Photograph by Levi Shinkle.)

In 2020, a new entrance was added to the park, part of the newest master plan. Included in this plan are hiking and biking interpretive trails, a new boat dock area handling fishers and tubers, enhanced landscaping, road improvements, and marketing for the 21st century. Supt. Kevin Skates is excited about the park joining the US Hot Springs Business and Trade Association. Many of that group's members have visited the park and appreciate the quality of the water and its health benefits. Hot Springs State Park will continue to provide many happy and healthy memories. (Photograph by Levi Shinkle.)

Consistent with our mission to preserve history on a local level, this book was printed in South Carolina on American-made paper and manufactured entirely in the United States. Products carrying the accredited Forest Stewardship Council (FSC) label are printed on 100 percent FSC-certified paper.

MADE IN THE USA